Clan
CAMPBELL

Extensively Revised

COMPILED BY
Alan McNie

CASCADE PUBLISHING COMPANY
Jedburgh, Scotland

Genealogical Research:
Research regrettably cannot be undertaken by the publisher. A non-profit organisation, The Scots Ancestry Research Society, 3 Albany Street, Edinburgh, undertake research for an agreed fee.

Alan McNie, 1983, extensively revised 1988
© Cascade Publishing Company
Rowandene, Belses, Jedburgh, Scotland

ISBN 0 9502637 0 2

Page 1 Explanation:
The illustrated tartan is worn by the present MacCailein Mor, just as it has been worn by many of his predecessors. This sett in darker tones has long had Campbell military associations. The motto on the crest badge is 'Do not forget' and the clan crest is the boar's head, with its original use likely going back to 5th century Argyll. The water colour rendering depicts Inveraray Castle, the present clan seat. Bottom right is the Bog Myrtle, one of the two Campbell plant badges, the other being Fir Club Moss.

Campbell Country

The map used below and on the following page is intended basically as a pictorial reference. It is accurate enough, however, to be correlated with a current map. The clan boundaries are only marginally correct. No precise boundaries were kept in early times and territories were fluctuating frequently.

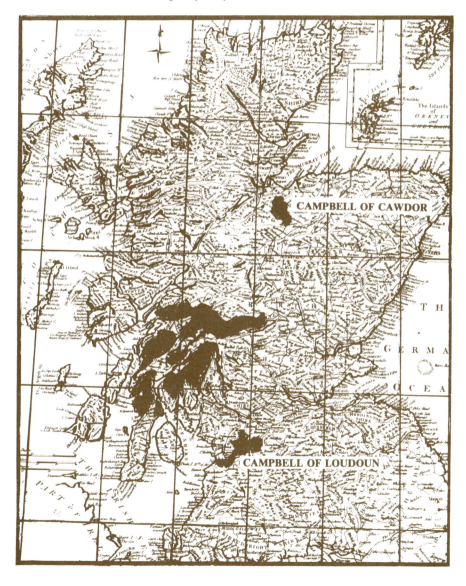

Campbell
CLAN MAP

1. **Ardmaddy Castle** An old fort enlarged by Lord Neil Campbell
2. **Ben Cruachan** Campbell battle cry is 'Cruachan'
3. **Campbeltown** Built to avoid paying feu duty
4. **Carrick Castle** Former stronghold now in ruins
5. **Castle of Barcaldine** 16th century Campbell outpost
6. **Dunstaffnage Castle** This MacDougall fortress fell to Campbells
7. **Inchchonnel Castle** First Campbell seat here
8. **Inveraray Castle** 15th century origins – now clan shrine
9. **Inverawe House** Ancestral home of Campbells of Inverawe
10. **Kilchrenan Church** Burial place of MacCailean Mor
11. **Kilchurn Castle** 15th century ruin built by Campbell of Glenorchy
12. **Strachur** Former MacArthur base
13. **Taymouth Castle** Former Breadalbane seat

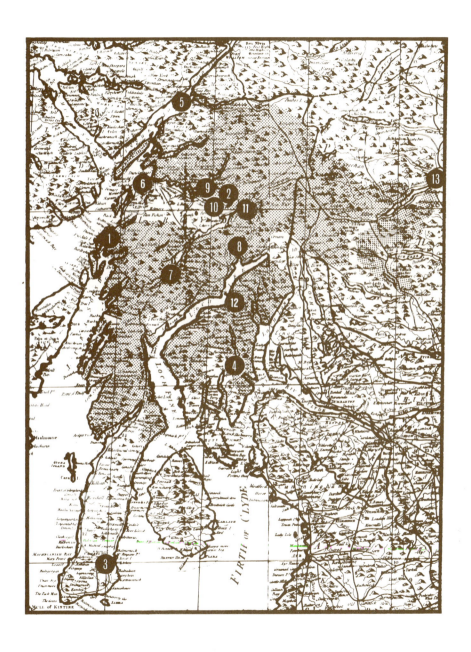

Auld Brig O' Doon *Campbell of Loudoun Country*

Loch Eck *Campbell of Argyll territory*

CLAN CAMPBELL

Condensed from Highland Clans of Scotland
George Eyre-Todd, 1923

Behind Torrisdale in Kintyre rises a mountain named Ben an Tuire, the "Hill of the Boar." It takes its name from a famous incident of Celtic legend. There, according to tradition, Diarmid O'Duibhne slew the fierce boar which had ravaged the district. Diarmid was of the time of the Ossianic heroes. The boar's bristles were poisonous, and a rival for his lady's love induced him to measure the hide with his naked feet. One of the bristles pricked him, and in consequence he died.

Diarmid is said to have been the ancestor of the race of O'Duibhne who owned the shores of Loch Awe, which were the original Oire Gaidheal, or Argyll, the "Land of the Gael." The race is said to have ended in the reign of Alexander III. in an heiress, Eva, daughter of Paul O'Duibhne, otherwise Paul of the Sporran, so named because, as the king's treasurer, he was supposed to carry the money-bag. Eva married a certain Archibald or Gillespie Campbell, to whom she carried the possessions of her house. This tradition is supported by a charter of David II. in 1368, which secured to the Archibald Campbell of that date certain lands on Loch Awe "as freely as these were enjoyed by his ancestor, Duncan O'Duibhne."

Who the original Archibald Campbell was remains a matter of dispute. By some he is said to have been a Norman knight, by name De Campo Bello. The name Campo Bello is, however, not Norman but Italian. It is out of all reason to suppose that an Italian ever made his way into the Highlands at such a time to secure a footing as a Highland chief; and the theory is too obviously one of the common and easy and nearly always wrong derivations of a name by mere similarity of sound. Much more probable seems a derivation from a personal characteristic in the usual Gaelic fashion. In this case the derivation would be from *cam beul,* "crook mouth," in the same way as the name Cameron is derived from *cam sron,* "crooked nose."

For a century and a half the MacArthurs of Strachur, on the opposite shore of Loch Fyne, appear to have been regarded as the senior branch of the clan. They certainly were the most powerful, and Skene in his *Highlanders of Scotland* says it is beyond question that they held the chiefship. Their claim may have been derived through marriage with a co-heiress of the O'Duibhnes. But with the execution of the MacArthur chief by James I. at Inverness in 1427 the Campbells were left as the chief family of the race of Diarmid.

Colin Mor Campbell of Lochow was knighted by Alexander III. in 1288, and it is from him that the succeeding chiefs of the race to the present day have been known as "Mac Cailean Mor." Colin the Great himself lies buried in the little kirkyard of Kilchrenan above the western shore of Loch Awe, where his descendant, a recent Duke of Argyll, placed over his resting-place a stone bearing the inscription, "To the memory of Cailean Mor, slain on the Straing of Lorne 13 – ." High on the hill ridge opposite, on the eastern side of the loch, a cairn marks the spot at which the doughty warrior, in the hour of victory, pursuing his enemy, MacDougall of Lorne, too far, was overcome and fell.

It was the son of this chief, Nigel or Neil Campbell, who, espousing the cause of Robert the Bruce, brought his family on to the platform of the great affairs of Scottish history. He befriended the king in his early wanderings, accompanied him in his winter's exile in Rachryn Island, and fought for him at Bannockburn, and as a reward he received in marriage Bruce's sister, the Princess Mary or Marjorie, while the forfeited lands of David de Strathbogie, Earl of

Atholl, were settled on their second son. From that hour the fortunes of the Campbells received hardly a check. Having helped, at the Bridge of Awe, to overthrow Bruce's enemies, the powerful Lords of Lorne and of Argyll, they proceeded piecemeal to supplant them and their kinsmen, the MacDonalds, and secure their lands. In some cases they compelled or induced the owners of these lands to assume the Campbell name.

In the reign of Bruce's son, David II., the next Chief of the Campbells, Sir Nigel's son, again played an important part. It was when the entire country was overrun by Edward Baliol and his English supporters. Robert, the young High Stewart, suddenly broke out of concealment in Bute, and stormed the strong castle of Dunoon. In this enterprise, which inspired the whole country to rise and throw off the yoke of the invader, the Stewart was splendidly helped by Colin Campbell of Lochow. As a reward the Campbell Chief was made hereditary governor of the stronghold, with certain lands to support the dignity. This grant brought the Campbells into conflict with the Lamonts, who were owners of the surrounding Cowal district, and in course of time they supplanted them in considerable possessions — the kirk of Kilmun, for instance, where they first begged a burial-place for a son whose body could not be carried through the deep snows to Inveraray and which remains the Argyll burying-place to the present hour; also Strath Echaig at hand, which was obtained from Robert III. as a penalty for the sons of the Lamont Chief beating off and slaying some young gallants from the court at Rothesay, who were trying to carry away a number of young women of Cowal.

Colin Campbell's grandson, another Sir Colin, further advanced his family by marrying a sister of Annabela Drummond, the queen of Robert III., and his son, Sir Duncan, married, first a daughter of Robert, Duke of Albany, son of Robert II. and Regent of Scotland, and secondly a daughter of Sir Robert Stewart of Blackhall, a natural son of Robert III. He was one of the hostages for the redemption of James I. from his English captivity in 1424, and at that time his annual revenue was stated to be fifteen hundred merks, a greater income than that of any of the other hostages. A further sign of his importance, he was made by James I. Privy Councillor, the King's Justiciary, and Lieutenant of the county of Argyll, and by James II., in 1445, he was raised to the dignity of a Lord of Parliament by the title of Lord

Loch Tay *Campbell country on left*

Dunstaffnage Castle

Campbell.

It was Lord Campbell's eldest son, Celestine, for whom a grave was begged for the Lamont Chief at Kilmun. The second son died before his father, leaving a son, Colin, who succeeded as second Lord Campbell, and became first Earl of Argyll, while the third son obtained the lands of Glenurchy, formerly a possession of the MacGregors, and founded the great family of the Campbells of Glenurchy, Earls and Marquesses of Breadalbane.

Hitherto the seat of the Campbells of Lochow had been the stronghold of Inchconnel, which still stands on the island of that name, amid the waters of the loch; but Glenurchy built for his nephew the first castle at Inveraray, which continued to be the headquarters of the family for four centuries. At the same time, during his absence abroad, his wife is said to have built for him, on an islet in the northern part of Loch Awe, the strong castle of Kilchurn, which remains to the present day one of the most picturesque features of the Highlands. Thenceforth the history of the Campbells of Breadalbane forms a separate and highly interesting chapter by itself.

Meanwhile the younger sons of each generation had become the founders of other notable families. The second son of Cailean Mor settling on Loch Tayside had founded the family of Campbell of Lawers, afterwards Earls of Loudoun, while the fourth son had been made by Robert the Bruce, Constable of Dunstaffnage, a post held by his descendant to the present day, and the fifth son, Duncan, is believed to have been ancestor of the Campbells of Inverurie, from whom sprang the families of Kilmartin, Southall, Lerags, and others. The third son of Sir Nigel Campbell had founded the house of Menstric, near Stirling. The second son of Sir Colin, the hero Dunoon, had become ancestor of the families of Barbreck and Succoth. The second son of Sir Colin, the fifth laird, and Margaret Drummond, was ancestor of the Campbells of Ardkinglas and their branches, the houses of Ardentinny, Dunoon, Skipnish, Blythswood, Shawfield, Dergachie, and others. And younger sons of Sir Duncan, first Lord Campbell, became ancestors of the Campbells of Auchenbreck, Glen Saddell, Eileangreig, Ormidale, and others.

Colin, second Lord Campbell, in view of his power and importance in the west, was made Earl of Argyll by James II. in 1457.

He was appointed Master of the Household of James III. in 1464. He acted as ambassador to England and France, and finally was made Lord High Chancellor of Scotland. By his marriage also he made conquest of another great lordship. His wife was the daughter and co-heir of John Stewart, Lord of Lorne, and by a forced settlement with the lady's uncle, Walter Stewart, he obtained in 1470 a charter of the lands and title of that lordship. Since that time the Galley of Lorne has by right of descent from the MacDougalls of Lorne, figured in the Campbell coat of arms. The Earl's second son founded the house of Campbell of Lundie, while his seven daughters made alliances with some of the most powerful nobles and chiefs in the country.

Archibald, second Earl of Argyll, was the leader of the vanguard of James IV.'s army at the disastrous battle of Flodden. At the head of the Highland clans and Islesmen he made the victorious rush with which the battle opened, but as the clansmen scattered to seize their plunder, the English cavalry charged on their flank, the Earl fell, and they were cut to pieces. Most notable of the families founded by his sons was that of Cawdor, who are Earls of Cawdor at the present time As Justiciar of Scotland the Earl did a service to Rose of Kilravock, for which he received the custody of Kilravock's granddaughter, the infant Muriel, heiress of the thanedom of Cawdor. The messenger sent to bring the child south had to fight a battle with her seven Cawdor uncles. Some suspicion of Campbell methods seems ot have been in the mind of the child's grandmother, old Lady Kilravock, for before handing her over to Campbell of Inverliver she thrust the key of her coffer into the fire and branded her on the thigh. Afterwards, when Inverliver was asked what he would think if the child that had cost him so much trouble should die, he is said to have replied, "Muriel of Cawdor will never die, so long as there is a red-haired lassie on the shores of Loch Awe." The Earl married Muriel to his third son, Sir John, who acquired Islay and played a considerable part in the affairs of his time. Among other matters he stabbed in his bed in Edinburgh, Maclean of Duart, who had exposed his wife, Cawdor's sister, on a rock in Loch Linnhe, to be drowned by the tide. From the second Earl descended the families of Ardchattan, Airds, Cluny, and others, and from his brother Donald, Abbot of Cupar, Keeper of the Privy Seal, came the Campbells of Keithock in Forfarshire.

Cawdor Castle

Loch Linnhe

Langside

Murder of Rizzio

Colin, third Earl of Argyll, was by James V. appointed Master of the Household, Lieutenant of the Border, Warden of the Marches, Sheriff of Argyll, and Justice-General of Scotland. His second son, John Gorm, who was killed at the battle of Langside, was ancestor of the families of Lochnell, Barbreck, Balerno, and Stonefield, and his daughter Elizabeth was the wife of the notorious Regent Earl of Moray, half-brother of Mary Queen of Scots.

Archibald, the fourth Earl, was appointed Justice-General of Scotland by James V., and was the first person of importance in Scotland to embrace the Protestant faith. He commanded the Scottish right wing at the battle of Pinkie in 1547. The fifth Earl, another Archibald, married a natural daughter of James V. His countess was the favourite half-sister of Queen Mary, was one of the Queen's supper-party at Holyrood when Rizzio was murdered, and acted as proxy for Elizabeth of England at the baptism of James VI. She and the Earl entertained the Queen at Dunoon Castle, and the Earl was commander of Mary's army at the battle of Langside. On that occasion, whether by sickness or treachery at the critical moment, he caused the loss of the battle to the Queen. He was afterwards appointed one of her lieutenants in Scotland, was a candidate for the regency, and became Lord High Chancelor.

His half-brother, Sir Colin Campbell of Boquhan, who succceeded as sixth Earl, was also, in 1579, appointed Lord High Chancellor. His son, Archibald, the seventh Earl, had a curious career. In 1594, at the age of eighteen, he was sent by James VI. to repress the Roman Catholic Earls of Errol and Huntly, and at the battle of Glenlivat was completely defeated by them.. He afterwards engaged in suppressing an insurrection of the MacDonalds, with whom his family had so long been at enmity, and distinguished himself by repressive acts against those other neighbours, the MacGregors, whom his family had for long been ousting, with the result that he nearly exterminated them. He is suspected of having instigated them to attack the Colquhouns, and after the battle of Glenfruin, it was he who secured the MacGregor Chief by first fulfilling his promise to convey him safely out of the country, and then, when he had crossed the Border, arresting and bringing him back to Edinburgh to be tried and executed. In his later years he went to Spain, became a Roman Catholic, and took part in the wars of Philip II. against the States of Holland.

His son, Archibald, the eighth Earl and first and last Marquess, for a time held supreme power in Scotland. Known as Gillespie Grumach, and as the Glied or squinting Marquess, he was at the head of the Covenanting Party, and had for his great rival and opponent the Royalist Marquess of Montrose. In 1633 he resigned into the hands of Charles I. the whole Justiciarship of Scotland except that over his own lands, and in 1641 was raised to the rank of Marquess of Argyll by that king. Nevertheless he was the chief opponent of Charles in the Civil War in Scotland. In the field he was no match for his brilliant opponent Montrose. At Kilsyth his army was completely defeated, and at Inverlochy, where he took to his barge and watched the battle from a safe distance, he saw the Royalist general cut his army to pieces and slay fifteen hundred of his clan. Among his acts in the war was the burning of the "Bonnie House o' Airlie," the home of Montrose's follower, the chief of the Ogilvies; for which act Montrose marched across the hills and gave Argyll's own stronghold, Castle Campbell in the Ochils above Dollar, to the flames. When Montrose was at last defeated at Philiphaugh, the captured Royalists were slain in cold blood in the courtyard of Newark Castle and elsewhere, and when Montrose himself was capured later, Argyll watched from a balcony in the Canongate as his enemy was led in rags up the street to his trial and execution. Then Argyll sent the army of the Covenant to destroy those old enemies of his family, the MacDonalds of Kintyre, and the MacDougalls of Dunolly, slaughtering the three hundred men of the garrison of Dunavertie, and burning the MacDougall strongholds of Dunolly and Gylen, while in Cowal he plundered the lands of the Lamonts, and had over two hundred of the clan butchered at Dunoon. When the young Charles II. came to Scotland in 1651 Argyll himself placed the crown on his head, and is said to have planned to get Charles to marry his own daughter, Anne. But after Cromwell's victory at Dunbar he assisted in proclaiming him as Protector, and engaged to support him. It could be no marvel, therefore, that at the Restoration in 1660 Charles II. resisted his advances, and that he was presently seized at Carrick Castle on Loch Goil, carried to Edinburgh, and tried and beheaded for his acts.

James Campbell, a younger half-brother of the Marquess, was

created Earl of Irvine in 1642, but as he had no family the peerage expired with him.

The Marquess' son, Archibald, was restored to the earldom and estates in 1663, but in 1681, having refused to conform to the Test Act, he was condemned and imprisoned in Edinburgh Castle. He made a romantic escape disguised as a page holding up the train of his stepdaughter, Lady Sophia Lindsay. But four years later, in concert with Monmouth's invasion of England, he landed in Loch Fyne, raised a force, and was marching upon Glasgow when, his force having dispersed, he was seized, disguised, at Inchinnan in Renfrewshire, and carried to execution at Edinburgh. A famous picture of the occasion commemorates "the last sleep of Argyll."

Of the Earl's four sons the second, John Campbell of Mamore, was forfeited for taking part in his father's expedition, but had his forfeiture rescinded at the Revolution in 1689, and represented Argyll in the Scottish Parliament in 1700 and Dunbarton in the first Parliament of the United Kingdom. The third son, Charles, forfeited and reinstated in the same way, represented Campbeltown in the Parliament of 1700. He married Lady Sophia Lindsay, the stepdaughter who had helped his father to escape from his first imprisonment in Edinburgh Castle. The fourth son, James, of Burnbank and Boquhan, in 1690 forcibly carried off Mary Wharton, an heiress of thirteen, and married her. The marriage was annulled by Act of Parliament, and one of Campbell's accomplices, Sir John Johnston, Bart., of Caskieben, was executed at Tyburn; but the chief perpetrator escaped to Scotland, to become a colonel of dragoons and represent Campbeltown in Parliament. He afterwards married the Hon. Margaret Leslie, daughter of Lord Newark.

Meanwhile the eldest son, Archibald, was one of the commissioners sent to offer the crown to William of Orange. The attainder against his father was reversed at the Revolution, and he was by King William created Duke of Argyll, with remainder to his heirs male whatsoever. He raised a Highland regiment which distinguished itself in King William's continental wars.

His son, John, the second Duke, was one of the greatest men of his time. A rival of Marlborough in the continental wars of Queen Anne, he commanded George I.'s army at the battle of Sheriffmuir

Castle Campbell *(P. 18)*

Inverarary Castle *Before conical roofs were added to the towers*

in 1715, and through his energy and ability preserved Scotland for that king. In 1719 he was made Duke of Greenwich, and in 1735 Field-Marshal commanding all the forces of the kingdom. A great statesman as well as a soldier, he is referred to by Pope:

> "Argyll, the state's whole thunder born to wield,
> And shake alike the senate and the field."

And it is he who figures in Sir Walter Scott's *Heart of Midlothian,* as the minister to whom Jeanie Deans appeals to secure the pardon of her erring sister, Effie. Among his honours he was a Knight of the Garter and a Knight of the Thistle, and his monument remains in Westminster Abbey.

As the Duke had no son his British titles died with him, and he was succeeded in the Scottish honours by his brother, Archibald, Earl of Islay. The third Duke had served under Marlborough and studied law at Utrecht. He became Lord High Treasurer of Scotland in 1705 and promoted the Union with England. He was made Lord Justice General in 1710, and Lord Register in 1714. He raised Argyllshire for George I. and fought under his brother at Sheriffmuir. He became Walpole's chief adviser in Scotland, and keeper successively of the privy seal and the great seal. For long he was the greatest man in Scottish affairs and it was he who rebuilt Inveraray Castle on its present site. In his time the strength of the clan was estimated at 5,000 fighting men, and it sent a contingent to fight against Prince Charles Edward at Culloden.

After him the dukedom went to his cousin, John Campbell of Mamore, son of the second son of the ninth earl. His second son was killed at the battle of Langfeldt in 1747 and his third son became Lord Clerk Register of Scotland. His eldest son, John, the fifth Duke, married Elizabeth Gunning, widow of the sixth Duke of Hamilton, one of the three sisters who were celebrated beauties at the court of George III. She was the wife of two dukes, and the mother of four, and was created Baroness Hamilton in her own right in 1776. Her second and third sons by the Duke of Argyll became successively sixth and seventh Dukes. The latter was a friend of Madame de Staël, who pictured him as Lord Nevil in her famous novel, *Corinne.* His son, George, the eighth Duke, was the distinguished statesman, orator, scholar, and author of Queen Victoria's time. Three times married, and three times Lord Privy Seal, he also filled the offices of Postmaster-General, Secretary for India, Chancellor of St Andrew's University, and Trustee of the British Museum. Among his honours he was K.G., K.T., P.C., D.C.L., L.L.D., and F.R.S., and among his writings were valuable works on science, religion, and politics. He bequeathed Iona Catherdal to the Church of Scotland.

He and his eldest son, John, the ninth Duke, inherited much of the personal beauty of their ancestor, Elizabeth Gunning, and when the latter in 1871 married H.R.H. the Princess Louise, fourth daughter of Queen Victoria, the pair were as distinguished for their fine looks as for their high rank. For ten years, as Marquess of Lorne, he represented Argyllshire in the House of Commons, and for a term he was Governor-General of Canada. He held many honours, and was the author of some interesting literary works.

Marquis of Lorne
Governor-General of Canada
9th Duke of Argyll

Princess Louise
daughter of
Queen Victoria

The Campbells of Breadalbane

Probably no Highland family has been so prolific in cadet branches of distinction as the great race of the Campbells. From the earliest date at which authentic history dawns upon their race they are found multiplying and establishing new houses throughout the land. The steps in the growth of this great house are in every generation full of interest, and involve in their narration no small part of the romance of Scottish history.

While the main stem of the family was carried on by Lord Campbell's second son's son, Colin, who became 1st Earl of Argyll in 1457, it was his third son, another Sir Colin, who founded the greatest of all the branches of the Campbells, that of Glenorchy and Glenfalloch, the head of which is now Earl of Breadalbane. So well had the heads of the house improved their fortunes that Lord Campbell was probably the richest noble in Scotland. When he became one of the hostages for the redemption of James I. in 1424, his annual revenue was stated to be fifteen hundred merks. He was well able, therefore, to endow his third son with the lands of Glenorchy and Glenfalloch in 1432.

Sir Colin Campbell of Glenorchy was one of the ablest men of his time. As guardian of his nephew, afterwards Earl of Argyll, he built for him the castle of Inverarary, and married him to the eldest daughter and co-heir of John Stewart, Lord of Lorne. He himself had married, first, Mariot, daughter of Sir Walter Stewart, eldest son of Murdoch, Duke of Albany, grandson of Robert II.; and on her death he married Margaret, the second daughter of the Lord of Lorne. By these marriages uncle and nephew not only acquired between them the great estates of the Stewart Lords of Lorne, but also placed upon their shields the famous lymphad, or galley, which betokened descent from the famous Somerled, Lord of the Isles.

Sir Colin, who was born about the year 1400, was a famous warrior, fought in Palestine, and was made a knight of Rhodes. The tradition runs that while he was away his wife built for him the castle of Kilchurn on its peninsula at the end of Loch Awe. He was so long absent that it was said he was dead, and the lady, like Penelope in the classic tale, was besieged by suitors. After long delays a neighbouring baron, MacCorquodale, it is said, forced her to a marriage. While the marriage feast was going on, a beggar came to the door. He refused to drink the health of the bride unless she herself handed him the cup. This she did, and as the beggar drank and returned it she gave a cry, for in the bottom lay Sir Colin's signet ring. The beggar was Sir Colin himself, returned just in time to rescue his wife.

After the assassination of James I. at Perth, Glenurchy captured one of the assassins, Thomas Chalmer of Lawers, on Loch Tay side, and as a reward he received a grant of the murderer's forfeited estate. His son and successor, Sir Duncan Campbell of Glenurchy, further added to the importance of his family by acquiring the estates of Glenlyon, Finlarig, and others on Loch Tay side. When he married Margaret, daughter of George, fourth earl of Angus, in 1479, he obtained with her a dowry of six hundred merks, and he fell with James IV. at Flodden in 1513.

His eldest son and successor, again, Sir Colin Campbell of Glenurchy, married Marjorie Stewart, daughter of John, Earl of Atholl, half brother of James II., her mother being Margaret Douglas, that Fair Maid of Galloway, who, as heiress of her ancient house, played such a strange romantic part in the story of her time.

Sir Colin, the youngest of the three sons who succeeded him, sat in the Scottish Parliament of 1560, and played an active part in furthering the Reformation. Till his time the lands of Breadalbane had belonged to the Carthusian Monastery at Perth founded by James I. Sir Colin first obtained a tack of these lands, and afterwards had them converted into a feu holding. He was a great builder of houses, and besides a noble lodging in Perth erected Edinample on Loch Earn, and in 1580 founded at the eastern end of Loch Tay the splendid family seat of Balloch, now known as Taymouth Castle. The site of this stronghold is said to have been settled in a curious way, Sir Colin being instructed in a dream to found his castle on the spot were he should first hear the blackbird sing on making his way down the strath. According to the family history written in 1598 he also added the corner turrets to Kilchurn Castle. Kilchurn and much of the other Breadalbane territory had once been possessed by Clan Gregor, but when feudal tenures came in, the chiefs of that clan had scorned to hold their land by what they termed "sheep-skin rights," and elected to continue

Loch Tay and Taymouth Castle

Kilchurn Castle

holding them by the ancient "coir a glaive," or right of the sword. As a result, when disputes arose they had no documents to show; the effort to vindicate their claims by the power of the sword got them into trouble; and the Campbells and other neighbours easily procured against them powers of reprisal which in the end led to the conquest and transferrence of most of the MacGregor territory. Sir Walter Scott put the plight and feelings of the clansmen concisely in his famouus lament:

> Glenorchy's proud mountain, Kilchurn and her towers,
> Glenstrae and Glenlyon no longer are ours;
> We're landless, landless, landless, Gregalach!

Accordingly we find in the Breadalbane family history that Sir Colin "was ane greate Justiciar all his tyme, throch the quhilk he sustenit that deidly feid of the Clan Gregor ane lang space. And besydis that, he causit execute to the death mony notable lymmars, and beheided the Laird of Mac Gregor himself at Keanmoir, in presence of the Erle of Atholl, the Justice Clerk, and sundrie uther nobillment."

Sir Duncan Campbell, the eldest son and successor of this redoubtable chief, is remembered in popular tradition by the names of "Black Duncan" or "Duncan with the cowl." Like his father he added greatly to his family possessions by acquiring feus of the church lands which were then extensively in the market as a result of the Reformation. At the same time he was perhaps the most enlightened landowner of his age. At any rate he was the first of Highland lairds to turn attention to rural improvement. Among other matters he was a great planter of trees, and also compelled his tenants to plant them. Many of the noble trees which still surround his stronghold of Finlarig, at the eastern end of Loch Tay, were no doubt of his planting. Like his father also he was a notable builder of strongholds, and besides Taymouth, Edinample, and Strathfillan, he possessed Finlarig, Loch Dochart, Achalader, and Barcaldine. From this partiality he obtained the further sobriquet of "Duncan of the Castles." When he began to build Finlarig someone is said to have asked why he was placing it at the edge of his property, and he is said to have replied, in characteristic Campbell fashion, that he meant to "birse yont." He was knighted by James I. in 1590; was made heritable keeper of the forest of Mamlorn in 1617, and afterwards Sheriff of Perth for life.

Finally, when the order of Baronets of Nova Scotia began to be created in 1625, he was one of the first to have the dignity conferred upon him. His first wife was Jean, daughter of John Stewart, Earl of Atholl, Chancellor of Scotland, and a few years ago the effigies of the pair were discovered on the under side of two stones which for centuries had been used as a footbridge across a ditch at Finlarig. At Finlarig are also still to be seen the gallows tree and the fatal pit in the courtyard, to which prisoners came from the Castle dungeon by an underground passage, to be gazed at by the laird's retainers before placing their head in the hollow at the side still to be seen, to be lopped off by the executioner. The heading axe of these terrible occasions was till 1922 preserved among other interesting relics at Taymouth Castle. Since 1508 the chapel at Finlarig has been the burying-place of the chiefs of the house.

Black Duncan's eldest son and successor, Sir Colin, was a patron of the fine arts, and encouraged the painter Jameson, the "Scottish Vandyck." His brother Robert, who succeeded him as third Baronet, and was previously known as "of Glenfalloch," represented Argyllshire in the Scottish parliaments of 1643, 1646, and 1647, the period of the civil wars of Charles I. and the exploits of the Marquess of Montrose.

This chief, the third baronet of Glenurchy, had by his two wives a family of no fewer than fifteen, of whom more anon. Meanwhile his eldest son's son, Sir John Campbell, fifth baronet of Glenorchy was to make history in more ways than one, both for his family and for the country. From his swarthy complexion he was known as Ian Glas. He was a clever and unscrupulous politician, and it was said of him that he was "cunning as a fox, wise as a serpent and slippery as an eel." By his first wife, the Lady Mary Rich, daughter of the first Earl of Holland, beheaded in 1649, he received a dowry of £10,000, and it is said that after the marriage in 1657, he conveyed her from London to the Highlands in simple fashion, the lady riding on a pillion behind her lord, while her marriage portion, which he made sure was paid in coin, was carried on the back of a strong gelding, guarded on each side by a sturdy, well-armed highlander. It was probably this money which helped him to one of the most notable actions of his career. At any rate it appears that among other investments he lent large sums of money to George, sixth Earl of Caithness. The Sinclairs

The McIan illustration of Campbell of Breadalbane as published (mid-19th century) in 'The Clans of the Scottish Highlands

have stories to tell, which may or may not be true, as to questionable methods by which these burdens of the Earl of Caithness were increased. One is that Charles II. obtained the earl's security for large sums, and then pledged it with Glenurchy. In any case in 1572 the Earl of Caithness found his debts overwhelming, and, being pressed by Glenurchy as his chief creditor, conveyed to him in wadset the whole property and titles of the Earldom, the possession of which was to become absolute if not redeemed within six years. The redemption did not take place, and on the death of the Earl, Glenurchy procured from the king in 1677, in right of his wadset, a new charter to the lands and title of Earl of Caithness. The heir to the Earldom also claimed the title and estates, and Glenurchy proceeded under legal sanction to enforce his rights by strength of arms. For this purpose he sent his kinsman, Captain Robert Campbell of Glenlyon, with a strong body of men, into the north. The Sinclairs also gathered in armed force, and the two parties came face to face, with a stream between them. Glenlyon is said by the Sinclairs to have used the strategy of sending a convoy of strong waters where he knew it would be captured by the Sinclairs, and at night, when the latter had enjoyed themselves not wisely but too well, the Campbells marched across the stream and utterly routed them. It was on this occasion that the Campbell piper composed the famous pibroch of the clan "Bodach na Briogais," the Lad of the Breeches, in ridicule of the Sinclairs, who wore that garment; and it is the event which is commemorated in the famous song "The Campbells are Coming." In the end, however, by the legitimate heir, George Sinclair of Keiss, the Campbells were driven out of the country, and Charles II., being at length persuaded of the injustice of his action, induced Glenurchy to drop the Caithness title, and compensated him in 1681 by creating him Earl of Breadalbane and Holland, with a number of minor dignities. Cunning as ever, Glenurchy procured the right to leave his titles to whichever of his sons by his first wife he should think proper to designate, and in the end, as a matter of fact, he passed over the elder of the two, Duncan, Lord Ormelie, who eventually died unmarried ten years after his father.

Glenurchy's first wife died in 1666, and twelve years later Glenurchy, probably by way of strengthening his claim to the Caithness title, married Mary, Countess Dowager of Caithness. This lady was

Glencoe

Killiecrankie

the third daughter of the notorious Archibald, Marquess of Argyll, who, strangely enough, like the father of Glenurchy's first wife, had been beheaded after the Restoration.

Possibly Breadalbane was inspired by his father-in-law's example to adopt sinister methods. At any rate we know that he was the chief mover in the transaction known in history as the Massacre of Glencoe. In this transaction he showed his usual cunning. Glencoe appeared a desirable addition to the estate. So also did Glenlyon. He had left Campbell of Glenlyon to bear the expense of the great Caithness expedition, and he now took advantage of Glenlyon's impecuniosity to induce him to act as his catspaw in the affair of Glencoe. In that affair Glenlyon had also a personal revenge to satisfy, for the MacDonalds of Glencoe, on their way home after the battle of Killiecrankie, had raided and thoroughly destroyed his lands. At any rate it was Captain Robert Campbell of Glenlyon, with a company of Campbells, who carried out the notorious massacre. What his feelings towards his chief may have been at a later day we do not know, when, upon riding into Edinburgh to redeem a wadset on his lands of Glenlyon only in the nick of time, he encountered his kinsman and chief in the act of closing the wadset and ousting him from his heritage. Such a personage was Ian Glas, first Earl of Breadalbane and Holland. The wily old chief lived till 1717. Two years before his death he sent 500 of his followers to join the Jacobite rising of the Earl of Mar, but escaped without serious consequences of the act.

The Second Earl of Breadalbane was Lord Lieutenant of Perthshire and a representative peer. In his time occurred the Jacobite rising of 1745, when it was reckoned that the Earl could put a thousand men into the field. The third Earl was a Lord of the Admiralty and an ambassador to the Danish and Russian courts. By his third wife the Earl had a son John, Lord Glenorcy, who died before him childless in 1771. His widow Willielma, daughter and co-heir of William Maxwell of Preston, was the famous Lady Glenorchy whose peculiar religious views induced her to found chapels for her followers in Edinburgh, Carlisle, Matlock and Strathfillan.

Some Campbell Associated Names

BANNATYNE (An old Bute family, Bannatyne or MacAmęlynes, located at Kames Castle, Bute.) Port Bannatyne, Bute, on Kames Bay, Bute, is today a small resort with the tower of Kames Castle overlooking the bay.

BURNES, BURNESS, BURNS (Originates from Scots brook or stream). Variations of this name common in Kincardineshire from early 14th century. One Campbell connection was Walter Campbell, a small estate owner near Taynuilt in Argyllshire who fled in 17th century to Kincardineshire (homestead of Robert Burns' ancestors before moving to Ayrshire) and assumed local name of Burnshouse. Robert Burns and his brother, Gilbert, changed their name from Burness to Burns (1786).

CADDELL, CADELL, CALDER, CAWDOR (Variants from same source. See pages 12-13).

DENOON, DENUNE This Campbell sept derives name from town of Denoon on Firth of Clyde. Sir Arthur de Denoon's name appears on charter relating to Monastery of Paisley in 1294. To aid their escape from justice, two Campbell brothers of Lochow, who had fled to Ross-shire, changed their name to Denune, their mother's maiden name. The name and its variants is still common in the area.

FISHER Robert dominus Piscator (Latin), burgess of Perth, 1292. Campbell associations show in the late 17th, early 18th centuries: Duncan Fisher, provost of Inveraray, involved in collection of debt, 1698; former Inveraray provost, James Campbell married to Mary Fisher, widow of merchant, 1717.

LOUDEN, LOUDON, LOWDEN, (From Loudoun in Ayrshire). Very early ties with Campbell through marriage. As a result of the marriage, charter was drawn up in 1315 bestowing on Sir Duncan Campbell and Sussana, his wife, all the lands of Loudon and Stevenston in Ayrshire. In 1601 a descendant, Sir Hugh Campbell of Loudon, was elevated to the peerage as Lord Campbell of Loudon. Sir John Campbell, the first Earl of Loudon, became Chancellor of Scotland in 1647.

MACARTHUR (ARTHUR) MACARTAIR, MACCARTER (From Old Irish "art—bear" and Gaelic "Artair" among other sources). Some but by no means all Arthurs have dropped prefix Mac. MacArthurs were a clan who reached their ascendency in the mid-14th century. They later became followers of Campbell. Duncan Makarturicht acted as witness concerning land charter, Stratherne, 1529. Douglas M'Airthour was sheriff clerk of Argyll, 1595.
Arthur, Bishop of Argyll, mentioned in connection with property sale, 1679. American General, Douglas MacArthur, had Scottish grandparents.

MACCONACHIE (From Gaelic "MacDhonnachaidh-son of Duncan") Although this has strong Robertson connections, Campbell sept associations include: MacConchie of Inverawe on Loch Etive, Campbell of Duntroon and Campbell of Glenfeochan. Angus M'Conchie witnessed holding of Craignish to Earl of Argyll, 1493. Fynlaw McAndoche witnessed holding of lands of Balnacand, 1514.

MACDIARMID, MACDERMONT, DERMID (From Gaelic "MacDhiarmid-son of Dermid") Originated from progenitor of the House of Lochow, Diarmid O'Dhunie. The MacDiarmids are associated with the Campbells of Breadalbane. Angus McDeirmid, Craignan, Glenlyon, charged by Margaret Campbell for not fulfilling marriage promise. Nemeas Mactarmayt was vicar of Kilchoman in Islay, 1427. Jhone Makhermyk was one of the mayors and officers of the sherrifdom of Perth, 1529.

MACGIBBON (From Gaelic "MacKibbon-son of Gibbon) The Campbell MacGibbons originated in the Glendaruel district of Argyllshire. Control of their lands was assumed about 1508 by Colin, Earl of Argyll. For aiding Clan Gregor, Robert Finla McGibbonesoun was fined, 1613. Duncan M'Gibbon was a volunteer in the Duke of Atholl's militia in Glenlyon, 1706. The MacGibbons are also associated with the Buchanans and Grahams.

MACIVER, MACIVOR, URE (From Gaelic MacIomhair, son of Ivar).
The founder of this sept was Ivor, son of Duncan, Lord of Lochow in the 13th century. Their territory included Asknish and sections of Cowal. The MacIvers were a separate clan for a lengthy period until the Argyll Campbells gained control. The encumbent clan chief, Duncan, was allowed to retain control of his estates, contingent upon a pledge of loyalty to the Campbells. In 1292 the lands of Malcolm McIvyr were incorporated into the sherrifdom of Lorne. Terlach McEuar acted as a charter witness at Carnasserie, 1436. Donald McUyver and Andree McUvyr were tenants of Ballegregane, Doune, 1419.

MACKELLAR (Apparently originates from Latin, Hilarius; in Gaelic as MacEalair, the son of Ealiar). At least as far back as 1470 the MacKellars owned Ardare, Glassary. Duncan MacKellar of Ardare, Glassary depute of Colin, Earl of Argyll, 1518.
Thomas M'Callar was procurator in Perth, 1550.

MACKESSACK, MACKESSOCK, MACKISSOCK (From Gaelic MacIosaig, son of Isaac) Lands in Ardere, Glastray were resigned by Mariot, daughter of Malmoria M'Kesek. The sept on the Moray Firth coast probably came with Colin, Earl of Argyll, who married daughter of the Regent Moray. In 1591 the name Makkesake appeared in records there. John M'Intheir was convicted in 1623 of letting M'Keissik's children die from hunger in Breadalbane. (Probably during famine).

MACNICHOL, MACNICOL (Originally derived from Greek, conquering people. As Middle Gaelic became M'Nicail, son of Nicol). No association with MacNichols or MacRiculs of Ross-shire. MacNichol of Succouth, Glenurcha was chief of the Lochawe MacNichols in Glenurcha. Thom Macnicoll appeared as witness in Glasgow, 1553. John M'Nicoll listed in Glenfallach, 1638 and Nicoll M'Nicoll in Galdanach, 1672.

MACNIVEN (From Gaelic MacNaoimhin, son of the holy one). The MacNivens, who were originally connected with the Macnaughtons had property about Lochawe. Later became Campbell dependents. Duncan M'Nicoll V'Nevin listed as Campbell of Barbeck follower in 1623. John M'Nivaine listed in muster-roll of laird of Glenurguhay, 1638. MacNiven Island is located in Loch Mor, Craignish.

MACTAVISH, TAWSE, THOMAS, THOMPSON, THOMSON (From Gaelic MacTamhais, a variant of MacThamhais, son of Tammas, Lowland Scots for Thomas). The MacTavishes, who are numerous in Argyllshire, are generally regarded as descendants of the Campbells. They likely originated from Taus Coir, an illegitimate son of a Lord of Lochow. Numerous variations have sprung from Mactavish, with many of these names having other origins. Doncan M'Thamais gave evidence concerning lands of Glassre in Argyllshire, 1355. Andrew Thomson, a Doune merchant, received a bond, 1694. Widow of William Thomson, received bequest of £200 in Ormsary, 1761.

ORR (Old Renfrewshire name, originally either from extinct placename or from Gaelic odhar, of sallow complexion). The numerous occurence of Orrs in Campbeltown, Kintyre since 1640 likely due to movement from Renfrewshire. John Or in Moy listed as Campbell of Cawdor family, 1578. Alexander Over, alias Robertson, in Connoch mentioned for receiving stolen goods belonging to Clan Gregor, 1613.

PATERSON, PATTERSON (Meaning Patricks or Patrickson). One of commonest Scottish surnames. The original home of the Clan Pheadirean (Patersons) was the north side of Loch Fyne, where they were formerly numerous. John Patersoune was Glasgow landholder in 1553. Letters were issued against Patrick Patersoune for defrauding king's customs at Irvine, 1524. Archibald Paterson, Campbeltown maltster, involved assignation of bond, 1733.

PINKERTON (Name from old barony of Pinkerton, near Dunbar, East Lothian).
Nicol de Pynkertoune of Haddingtonshire rendered homage in 1296. Felicia Pyncartoun was involved in property transaction in Glasgow, 1552. Allan Pinkerton, the famous American detective was born in Glasgow, 1819.

TAWSE, THOMAS, THOMPSON, THOMSON (See MacTavish)

URE (See MacIver)

Some Clan Notables

Robert Burns' Highland Mary was Mary Campbell of Auchnamore, near Dunoon.

Campbell, William *(1862-1938)* Of Scottish ancestry this outstanding American astronomer designed the Mills spectograph and played a key role in the foundation of astrophysics.

Campbell, Norman *(1880-1949)* This Dumbartonshire experimental physicist had a particular interest in the electrical discharge in gases. He is, however, best remembered as a philosopher of science where he had many original concepts.

Campbell, Sir Malcolm *(1885-1945)* Of Highland stock this racing enthusiast of cars and speedboats — each named Bluebird — held many world records on land and water. The wartime Spitfire engine was developed from his racing engine.

Campbell, Donald *(1921-1967)* Son of Sir Malcolm (q.v.) Donald propelled another generation of Bluebirds on land and water at record speeds. His relentless quest for even faster racing led to his death when he was killed in a 300 miles-per-hour crash attempting to break his own record on Lake Coniston in the Lake District.